Original title:
The Moon's Mood Swings

Copyright © 2025 Creative Arts Management OÜ
All rights reserved.

Author: Rafael Sterling
ISBN HARDBACK: 978-1-80567-844-1
ISBN PAPERBACK: 978-1-80567-965-3

Melancholy Above the Horizon

A silver smile lights the night,
But oh, it frowns, what a sight.
Twirling clouds play peek-a-boo,
Is that laughter or a boo-hoo?

Hanging high like a rubber ball,
Wobbling round, oh what a fall.
Sometimes bright, sometimes shy,
Are you soaring or just a lie?

Glistening Lullabies in Isolation

Softly sings a glowing tune,
Like a child in a brightened moon.
Whispers float on night's cool air,
Who knew giggles could be rare?

Silly shadows dance away,
Swirling joy in a moonlit play.
Do you trip or do you glide?
Such a quirky cosmic ride!

Phases of a Whispering Heart

She's a diva in a gown of light,
Winks at lovers, just out of sight.
Yet sometimes dims, a sulky pout,
Caught in dreams, she spins about.

Look at her phases, such a tease,
Playing tricks with giggles and breeze.
Dancing wildly, then she hides,
The way she plays, oh how she bides!

Night's Gentle Caress and Fury

She tickles stars from afar,
Yet throws a fit, what a bizarre!
Tugging tides with a playful hand,
Cranky moods on her silver strand.

Furious flashes through the dark,
A shining puzzle, where's the spark?
Silly games beneath her glow,
A cosmic jester stealing the show!

A Glimpse of Solitude

A bright light peeks, then hides away,
It plays the game of night and day.
One moment giggles, then it frowns,
While shadows dance in silver gowns.

It blushes pink, then goes all blue,
As crickets sing their midnight tune.
A solitary friend, with moods so wild,
Beware, it tempers like a child.

Radiance of Remorse

Oh, shining orb, you sly sly tease,
You beam so bright, then dim with ease.
This fickle friend brings sparkles and fright,
As comets laugh and zip in flight.

With every twinkle, tales unfold,
Of midnight snacks and secrets told.
A guilty glow, it waves goodbye,
Then comes back with a gleeful sigh.

Silvered Dreams

Up high, it struts, with beams of flair,
Twirling clouds like a billionaire.
Cascading light, it makes us see,
A shimmering dance of reverie.

Each wink evokes a playful cheer,
Yet hides a giggle we might hear.
While dreamers float in slumber's lap,
The sly giggles in a silvery wrap.

Celestial Tantrum

A fantastical face, all craters and light,
Pouts like a child when it's not in sight.
It throws a fit, then blinks so bright,
While stars above roar with delight.

Swirling clouds and occasional gleams,
It's a toddler in space with goofy dreams.
Chasing dreams, then pulling a caper,
This breathless sky's a cosmic paper.

An Orbit of Oscillation

Round and round, our friend does glide,
One moment bright, and then she hides.
A playful wink, a shining grin,
Next, she's grumpy, won't let us in.

Her phases swing like a jolly kite,
Making nights jumpy, a silly sight.
She throws a party in the sky,
Then sulks away with a pout and sigh.

Chasing Reflections

Catch a glimpse of her shining face,
In the lake, she picks up the pace.
Then she splashes, making us laugh,
Playing games like a bubbly calf.

She hides behind clouds, oh, what a tease,
Then reappears, as bright as you please.
Oh fickle friend, we await your glow,
Each night a tale, a silly show.

Harmonies in Shadows

With a flicker here and a shimmer there,
She juggles shadows, a cosmic flare.
In a laugh or two, she spins around,
A giggle escapes, a teasing sound.

One moment shy, the next so bold,
Telling stories of mischief untold.
In the twilight dance, she does prance,
A partner in mischief, ready to chance.

Silvery Sighs

Oh, the giggles that you hide,
Creating nighttime's sneaky tide.
With a twirl, you cast your light,
Then huff and puff, just out of spite.

You smirk and glow, a celestial cheer,
Then sulk away, oh dear, oh dear!
Your laughter echoes across the bay,
A playful spirit, who loves to play.

Lunar Whispers in Twilight

When night falls, she wears a grin,
A silver smile, let the giggles begin.
But wait, she frowns, oh what a tease,
Turning shy behind a frilly breeze.

Her glow can wane, like a shy little sprite,
Hiding behind clouds, oh what a sight!
A twinkle here, a sparkle there,
Just like her, we laugh and stare.

Celestial Tides of Emotion

At times, she's a dancer, hips swaying wide,
Then suddenly sulky, it's quite the ride!
Like a playful child, she hops and skips,
Then sadly pouts, giving cheeky quips.

Her laughter echoes through the night's embrace,
But then she's gone—vanished without a trace!
"Where'd you go?" we cry in vain,
"I was just here!" she shouts in disdain.

Silver Shadows in Flux

One minute she's full, the next she's shy,
Crying, laughing, with each passing sigh.
Her phases crack jokes, make us all cheer,
Then she rolls her eyes, as if we're not here.

A crescent grin, then a frown so round,
Her antics leave giggles all over the ground.
Oh, what a show this gal likes to throw,
Always upending the night's sweet flow.

Changing Faces of Night

With a wink and a giggle, she plays her part,
Transforming the sky, a true work of art.
Then with a grump, she just might retreat,
Leaving us chuckling, oh isn't she sweet?

From waxing bright to waning meek,
Her moods swing wildly, we can't help but peek.
Like a comedian with no set routine,
She beams and she pouts, always unseen.

Dreaming in Moonlight

In silver robes she winks with glee,
A playful trickster, can't you see?
She pulls the tides, makes them dance,
As crickets chirp, they take a chance.

With cheese and crackers, her favorite fare,
She giggles softly, a nighttime dare.
Her glowing face, a party's thrill,
While owls hoot loud, she sits quite still.

Beware the wolves, they howl for fun,
While dancing shadows play and run.
She juggles clouds and stars galore,
Inviting all to join her floor.

So if you peek up late tonight,
And catch her grin, you'll hold on tight.
Laughing softly in her light,
She brings a cheerful delight in flight.

Mysteries of the Night

She checks her watch—oh, what a sight!
A glowing face, so full of light.
With secrets shared from star to star,
She whispers tales of near and far.

Her fuzzy clouds like cats on her lap,
She twirls around, setting each trap.
For shadows play games, a riddle's tease,
While shooting stars wink in the breeze.

"Hey, look at that!" the crickets cheer,
As she swaps her glow for a mischievous sneer.
A wink and a nod, she takes a bow,
Then changes her dress—oh, what a wow!

So welcome the night with glee and jest,
For in her laughter, we're truly blessed.
A nighttime show, a fun delight,
In the shining glow of the starry night.

Lunar Lullabies

In the night, she makes a fuss,
Chasing stars, she causes a ruckus.
One moment bright, then oh so shy,
Winking at dreams that dance on high.

With a giggle, she spills her light,
Turning shadows into delight.
Hiding behind clouds, she plays peek-a-boo,
Making wishes come true for me and you.

Her playful glow dims for a joke,
Hiding behind and making us choke.
Lighting up blunders with a smirk,
As owls hoot and the night goes berserk.

What's this game of hop and skip?
The stars applaud her little trip.
A cosmic dance on velvet seas,
Tickling the night with whimsical breeze.

Lighthearted Darkness

In a tutu made of starlight beams,
She twirls around, shattering dreams.
First a grin, then a silly pout,
Flipping the night's script inside out.

She plays tricks with shadows that creep,
Making all the sleepy folks leap.
One silly wink, a magical scene,
Turning dark into something pristine.

With each face, she coaxes a chuckle,
A grin so big it makes you buckle.
Painting the skies with laughter's glow,
Knocking on dreams, saying, "Let's go!"

In this dusky comedy act,
She flips, she flops, never lacks.
Illuminating the funny in fright,
She revels in our giggles tonight.

Shifting Silhouettes

A shadow dance, a playful tease,
Swaying softly in a gentle breeze.
One day round, next day slim,
Grinning wide with a cheeky whim.

Darkness wears a funny hat,
Juggling stars, how about that?
With a flip of her glowing hair,
The cosmos giggles without a care.

Like a performer in a grand parade,
She shapes the night like a game played.
One minute elegant, the next absurd,
She loves a laugh; that's her word.

In this fleeting cosmic show,
She swirls and twirls, a true pro.
Leaping high, then dropping low,
Her joyous antics steal the show!

Tidal Tempests

Whimsical waves, a splashy spree,
She turns the tides, oh what glee!
From geometric curls to rabid swirls,
In the ocean of stars, laughter unfurls.

As the tides dance with a wink,
She dips and dives, making us think.
"Who needs calm when chaos is fun?"
As the waves bob and laugh, they run!

Blowing kisses to the sailors wise,
She stirs the night with her giddy sighs.
Bubbles of mirth arise, explode,
Creating giggles on every road.

A tempest of jests beneath the light,
As shadows tease the serene night.
With every surge, she plays a tune,
Tickling the tides till the break of noon!

Glistening Gloom

In silver beams she winks and grins,
Then sulks behind a veil of sins.
Her laugh is bright, her pouts are loud,
A cheeky star among the crowd.

Her glow becomes a playful tease,
Amidst the night, she seems to please.
One minute bright, the next she frowns,
Creating chaos in sleepy towns.

Sorrowful Serenities

She sighs a lot, our hefty friend,
While causing tides to twist and bend.
With every phase, a brand-new tale,
Her drama's ripe—a whimsical gale.

At times she hides, then peeks with cheer,
A mystery wrapped in silver veneer.
A jovial trickster in the skies,
Luring gazes with her glowing lies.

Gleeful Glow

She dances bright, a sparkly tease,
And giggles soft with playful ease.
Her laughter echoes in the breeze,
As crickets play their nightly keys.

With a wink, she spins around,
A jester on her starry ground.
One moment soft, the next she's wild,
Her silly games leave lovers smiled.

Echoes in the Dark

In shadows deep, she throws a jest,
With twinkling eyes, she loves to test.
One minute shy, the next a queen,
Her playful jive, a lovely scene.

With secrets spun in midnight's embrace,
She crafts her whims, a merry chase.
As giggles dance upon the night,
Our lunar friend, a comedic sight.

Celestial Secrets and Starlit Longing

Up high in the sky she dances,
With giggles that sparkle, and wild romps.
Sometimes she's shy, then she prances,
Hiding behind clouds, giving little chomp.

With a wink here and a grin there,
She juggles her glow like a silly clown.
Round and round, without a care,
Chasing her shine in a shimmering gown.

Fractured Light

Look at her smile, then catch her frown,
Twinkling tricks in the darkened sky.
She flips her switch from a dance to a frown,
Shining wide as she lets out a sigh.

Sometimes she slips, a slip 'n' slide,
And beams like a sun in a lazy spree.
A cheeky flirt on a magical ride,
Playing hide and seek with the wandering bee.

Whirling Dreams

In a whirl of light, she twirls with glee,
Spinning tales of laughter, oh so bright.
A riddle of beams, just you and me,
Dancing through dreams on a starlit night.

When she pirouettes, shadows prance,
Follow her lead, the starry leash.
We stumble and giggle, lost in the chance,
While she teases us with a playful speech.

Mystic Rhythms in a Celestial Sea

Floating high in her cosmic grace,
She jests with stars that wink and twirl.
A playful glance, a cheeky face,
Off she goes, a mischievous swirl.

With a lantern in hand, she shows the way,
To whimsical shores where dreams arise.
Drifting in laughter, come what may,
Is it night or day? Who's to surmise?

Reflections of Euphoria and Sorrow

One moment she chuckles, the next she weeps,
Tears of silver, laughter of gold.
In cycles she dances, her secret keeps,
As the world beneath her stops to behold.

Echoing joy, then a sigh so deep,
Jokes that tickle and stories that borrow,
A riddle of light, in shadows so steep,
Forever changing, a mix of sorrow.

Whims of the Moonlit Sky

At times she winks, a cheeky tease,
Her silver beams bring total ease.
Then pouts like clouds with thunderous might,
Stomping her feet in a starry night.

She giggles bright, a playful sight,
While shadows dance in sheer delight.
With a twist, she pulls a face,
Leaving Earth in a comical chase.

Once serene, then frowning low,
A jester's heart in cosmic show.
We laugh aloud at her wild whims,
As night unfolds in glittering trims.

In wild waltz she likes to play,
With every phase she's quite the display.
A fabulous queen in her own right,
Forever flipping the realms of night.

A Dance of Light and Dark

She pirouettes through velvet skies,
With twinkling stars and muffled sighs.
One moment bright, the next, a shade,
In her grand ball, the fun's parlayed.

Holding hands with the friendly sun,
A playful spar where shadows run.
With silly faces, they do compete,
In turn and whirl, a dance so sweet.

Her laughter spills on sleepy towns,
While sleepy cats in windows frown.
For every chuckle, a gleeful shout,
As moonbeams frolic all about.

A spin, a twirl, she loves the jest,
From crescent curls to full-blown fest.
In this ballet of night and light,
She keeps us giggling till morning's bright.

Crescendo of Craters

With craters deep as playful pits,
A bumpy ride on her moonlit wits.
She pokes fun with riddles galore,
As we gaze up, our imaginations soar.

Each crater tells a story, it seems,
Of cosmic pies and stardust dreams.
Her face, a canvas of zany art,
Painted with whimsy, she plays her part.

Don't you dare call her too serene,
For she's the queen of silly routine.
With a wink and nod, she spins a tale,
As midnight revelers dance, prevail.

Her crescendo rises, laughter ignites,
Punctuating the stillness of nights.
In her craters, a joy so bright,
The universe giggles in sheer delight.

Ebbing Reflections of Selene

She rises high, then dips away,
With goofy grins on display.
In moonlit games, she loves to tease,
Her lighthearted glow puts hearts at ease.

In whispers soft, she plays peek-a-boo,
With shadowy friends, the night's crew too.
Adventures shared with every glance,
In a twinkling waltz, they prance and dance.

Her tides might pull, but spirits stay,
In this lunatic ballet, hooray!
With comical gestures, hers is the show,
Shining wide with a radiant glow.

So here's to the gleeful ebb and flow,
To the laughter of skies, a merry glow.
In her mischief, we find delight,
A jovial journey through the night.

A Dance Among Stars

Under silver beams, she twirls and spins,
With every phase, she giggles and grins.
A crescent smile or a roundly pout,
She bounces along, full of playful doubt.

As comets laugh, they pass her by,
Shooting stars wink; she's the apple of the sky.
In a full-blown rave, she shines so bright,
Bopping to the blues of the starry night.

The Enigmatic Glow

In peek-a-boo games behind the clouds,
She chuckles softly, drawing merry crowds.
One moment glowing, the next she's shy,
A cheeky glimmer, all while asking why.

Eclipses come and steal her light,
But she throws a party, oh what a sight!
With shadows dancing, her laughter flows,
A cosmic jest; only she truly knows.

Swaying Shadows

Her shadow stretches, then quickly shrinks,
As craters giggle and stardust winks.
She sways with whims, it's a celestial jam,
Dancing delightfully like a cosmic dram.

Fickle and funny, with every phase,
She curtsies low, then starts to graze.
With each gentle sway, laughter erupts,
In the theater of night, she leaps and jumps.

Light and Lament

In the still of night, she feigns a sigh,
A flicker of sadness but never goodbye.
Her beams play tricks, they're not what they seem,
Worry not, dear friends; it's all just a dream.

She casts her glow on the lonely bard,
While cracking wise like an old heartfelt card.
With jest and joy, she'll light up your night,
Dancing through tears, yet shining so bright.

Whims of the Night Sky

In a cloak of silver twirls,
The night giggles and swirls,
Balloons of clouds float high,
While stars wink and comply.

One moment a grin, the next a frown,
Dancing shadows merge and drown,
Crickets chirp in playful tricks,
As night makes its quick fix.

A tickle of winds, a shiver of chills,
Moonbeams drip like candy spills,
With laughter littering the dark,
As night clouds form a playful arc.

In this sky, giggles blend,
With the twist and twirl, they send,
A serenade from the above,
In the cosmos, jokes we love.

Glimmers of Ambivalence

Oh, the silver sphere up high,
Winks its eye with a sigh,
A grin that flips with a spin,
Disguised mischief held within.

One minute bright, then shy it goes,
Jesting with its lunar prose,
Ticklish beams in stealthy flight,
Chasing shadows through the night.

With every chuckle, clouds parade,
Bringing smiles that quickly fade,
A giggling haze that paints the sky,
As stars play tag and fly so high.

Beneath the glow of silver light,
Laughter echoes through the night,
A cosmic jester in the dark,
Playing tricks that leave a mark.

Starlit Stories

In a blazing comedy show,
Stars spin tales that ebb and flow,
With each giggle, a spark ignites,
Weaving fables of funny nights.

A crescent sneers, a full moon beams,
As starlight dances in silly dreams,
Whispers swirl in the vibrant air,
Where laughter blossoms everywhere.

Fleeting shadows join the jest,
In wrinkled clouds, they find their rest,
Stories wrapped in twinkling glow,
As the universe puts on its show.

High above, the humor reigns,
In this comedy of cosmic chains,
Every twinkle, a chuckle or two,
In starlit stories, laughter rings true.

Lunar Reflections

Bouncing beams and goofy grins,
The night reveals its thickest skins,
In playful hues, the shadows play,
Shooting stars with pranks to relay.

Puppies chase the glowing orbs,
While the night hums and burbles,
Caught in a bubble of loose delight,
Where laughter tugs all through the night.

With a wink, the dark might tease,
Cranking up the suspense with ease,
As giggles shimmy on quiet ground,
Echoes of whimsy all around.

An encore of fun on a silver stage,
Where the night showcases every page,
In lunar reflections, jokes spread wide,
As twinkling lights embrace the ride.

Soft Sighs of Night

In the dark, a big round face,
Winking down with endless grace.
Sometimes coy, and then so bright,
Poking fun at stars in flight.

Giggles bounce from cloud to cloud,
Secret chuckles, oh so loud.
While wise owls furrow their brow,
And wonder why she's silly now.

A silver spoon in cosmic pie,
Swaying gently, oh my my!
Points to lovers, sighs and swoons,
Teaching shadows how to croon.

As she dances, tricks unfold,
Pouting like a child so bold.
Her funny moves cause starlit glee,
In nightly jest, eternally.

Celestial Contradictions

A cheeky grin, she spins around,
One moment shy, the next unbound.
She flips the switch, lights up the night,
Then grumbles low like she's uptight.

Whispers tell of cosmic games,
Chasing stars while blanketing flames.
Her playful quirks cause all to stare,
Unruly joy floats through the air.

A giggle here, a sulk there too,
How is it that she's feeling blue?
The sky erupts with colorful swirls,
As laughter dances, twirls, and whirls.

Beneath her gaze, the night reveals,
Glimpses of truth amid the reels.
She jests and teases, gives a wink,
A riddle wrapped in lunar ink.

Melancholy's Embrace

To ponder deep in twilight's glow,
She softens into shades of woe.
Yet, with a smirk and jaunty flare,
She tickles dreams that float in air.

With pensive sighs, she cradles night,
And then erupts in beams of light.
Wistful whispers weave through trees,
In-between her playful sneeze.

A dance of joy, then quick retreat,
She chops the silence with a beat.
Is she sad or just confused?
With each glow, her heart's amused.

Cloaked in mystery, she writes her tale,
With silly quirks that never pale.
Moonlit giggles in the black,
Always ready with a comeback.

Waxes and Wanes

She rises high, a shining grin,
Then dips away, where to begin?
Calls for dances, makes a scene,
Fades into her night-time gleam.

Oh, what a trickster she can be,
Pulling jokes from infinity.
A cosmic tease, she's sly and spry,
Changing shapes up in the sky.

With each new phase, a fresh disguise,
Hiding smiles in celestial lies.
Heartbeat synced with nighttime's chime,
She sings her song, a funny rhyme.

By dawn, she'll leave a giggling trace,
As if to say, "I've won this race!"
But don't be fooled, she'll be back soon,
To play again beneath the moon.

Reflective Radiance

Up high she glows, a silver spoon,
Whispering secrets to the night soon.
One moment bright, the next a pout,
Dancing with stars, then filled with doubt.

She peeks through clouds, a shy little tease,
Winks at the Earth, just to please.
"Oh, do you see me?" she giggles with glee,
Then hides away like a child at three.

With a flick of her light, she plays games of chase,
Reminds us of laughter with a soft embrace.
Some nights a beacon, at times a small light,
What a comedian, under black velvet night.

Is she a flirt, or simply coy?
Her jests bring us laughter, like a child's toy.
In the night sky, oh what a scene,
Our silvery jester, looking quite serene.

Emotions on a Horizon

A glow in the sky, oh what a show,
One minute smiling, then down she goes.
Like a friend at a party, shifts from high to low,
Changing her vibe, with every wind blow.

Draped in clouds, sassy and bold,
Peering through gaps, her stories unfold.
She dips and she dives, like a boat on the sea,
"Catch me if you can!" she giggles with glee.

One night she's a crier, with tears all around,
Next, she's a joker, with giggles profound.
A flicker of cheer, then a frown in her beam,
A cosmic comedian, lost in a dream.

Caught in her antics, we just can't resist,
Betwixt her moods, she's hard to dismiss.
What a dear friend, so fickle yet bright,
In shades of the dark, she brings pure delight.

Flux and Flow

From crescent to full, she's got quite a flair,
With moods that could fill a clown's airy lair.
Some nights she winks, like a playful tease,
Other times frowning, like a chilled summer breeze.

Swings like a pendulum, oh what a sight,
Twirling and leaping, a joyful delight.
She might just throw a fit, then giggle and spin,
Right under the stars, let the fun begin!

One night she's shy, whispering low,
Next she's a party, putting on a show.
With a round, jolly face, she beams like the sun,
Oh, what a spectacle, this mood dance is fun!

Her laughter echoes through the vastness of space,
All with a chuckle, a wink on her face.
We join in her game, what a wild ride,
With this whimsical glow, let's all glide!

Celestial Serenade

Under stars she plays, a twinkly queen,
Sometimes elegant, other times obscene.
In a sparkle and shimmer, she jests and jibes,
With a laugh through the cosmos, a giggle that vibes.

Lights flicker wildly, a playful ballet,
She's fun on the edge, in her cosmic sway.
One moment serene, the next in a twist,
Schadenfreude glows, like a light in the mist.

Her moods pirouette, never well planned,
Just like a kitten, she leaps from the hand.
In a laughter-filled riddle, she dances with stars,
Her joy is contagious, even beyond Mars.

So here's to the night, a whimsical muse,
In gowns made of silk, she'll never amuse.
With giggles and light, through the dark she'll sail,
Our wily night friend, with stories to tell.

Ethereal Encounters

In the night sky, a cheeky grin,
Laughing stars, where dreams begin.
A wink from clouds, a little tease,
While shadows shuffle under trees.

A giggle bounces off the lake,
Water ripples, knowing what's at stake.
Crickets cheer in silly tune,
Chasing tails of the merry moon.

Transforming silver into gold,
Whispered secrets, tales retold.
She plays hide and seek with light,
A jester in the velvet night.

With every phase, a playful jest,
In her glow, we're truly blessed.
So raise a glass to her bright face,
In her glow, we find our place.

Whirls of Light

Spinning rays in wild delight,
Slippers on, we dance all night.
Sparkling smiles in the air,
Swirls of joy without a care.

An impish laugh from above,
Winking down with playful love.
Chasing shadows, twirling high,
While night whispers a lullaby.

A game of tag with the stars,
Who needs luck? We've got ours!
Round and round, the laughter flows,
As our heartbeat ebbs and grows.

In the moon's embrace, we sway,
Glowing softly, come what may.
Her whimsy lights our endless gleam,
Together lost in a silly dream.

Dancing with Dusk

When twilight paints the sky with glee,
We twirl beneath, so light and free.
Balloons of laughter drift away,
As stars peek out to join the play.

A jolly jig upon the grass,
Where shadows dance as moments pass.
With every beat, the world aligns,
In a tango of silly signs.

Here comes a flicker, here comes a grin,
As dusk and light begin to spin.
A comedy of glow and dark,
In this surreal, sparkling park.

With every twirl, a giggle grows,
Echoing through moonlit shows.
So come along, embrace the night,
For whimsy reigns in soft moonlight.

Crystalline Echoes

In crystal-clear night, laughter rings,
Echoes dance on fairy wings.
A shimmer here, a sparkle there,
With every ripple, whimsy's rare.

Jugs of starlight spill and roll,
While giggles crowd around the shoal.
Every splash, a funny face,
Reflecting joy in this wondrous space.

Drifting dreams on a silver tide,
With twinkling secrets they abide.
Each blink a joke, each sigh a cheer,
The night is wise, the dawn is near.

So lift your voice, let laughter rise,
In the stillness, hear the sighs.
For in this realm of glimmering beams,
Reality bends to our wild dreams.

Lunar Labyrinths

In a night so bright, she grins,
Chasing shadows, making spins,
Crickets chuckle, stars align,
What a funny waltz, divine!

But alas, a cloud does tease,
She pouts, then dances with the breeze,
A giggle here, a sly wink there,
Oh, the antics she can wear!

With each phase, a sudden twist,
Waxing, waning, not to miss,
She juggles dreams and beams of light,
Who knew she'd be such a sight?

Yet in her games, we find delight,
A playful laugh, the world's invite,
For in her glow, we love to play,
With every change, she steals the day!

The Heart's Constellation

A wink from her makes hearts collide,
Romance thrived, on this joyride,
But soon enough, she shifts her grace,
Now mismatched socks, a silly face!

She lights up dreams, then dims the scene,
Bowling with a comet, truly keen,
Her laughter echoes through the night,
In her quirks, the stars seem bright!

Playing tag with shadows bold,
Stories of love and laughter told,
Through cosmic spins and playful grace,
She weaves a smile, a warm embrace!

And just like that, she flirts anew,
Chasing stardust, a playful view,
Her heart's constellation, none can miss,
In every twinkle, a cosmic kiss!

Flickering Fragments

A glimmer here, a flicker there,
She tosses glitter in the air,
Bounding forth with cheer and glee,
A sight that begs you, 'Come and see!'

But don't be fooled, she can be sly,
Hiding behind a cloud to cry,
Then suddenly, with a burst of cheer,
She's back, making the world sincere!

Her beams like twinkling fireflies,
Dancing around with no goodbyes,
Yet when it's time to turn around,
Her laughter bounces, lost and found!

From giggles soft to howls of fun,
In her silly games, we all have won,
A game of chase, a fleeting glance,
Oh, what a spark in this cosmic dance!

Celestial Contemplation

On a quiet night, she starts to scheme,
Twirling thoughts, doodling a dream,
Shadows slip, as starlights play,
Tickling ideas, in her display!

But wait, what's this? A frown appears,
Grumpy clouds, they bring her fears,
Yet swiftly she laughs, flips a cap,
'Don't you dare! I'll make a map!'

From moody blues to shades of gold,
Her antics never get too old,
For in each phase, she finds a tune,
With giggles bright, we chase the moon!

So here she shines, a cheeky jest,
Teaching us all how to zest,
In her glow, we find our way,
With laughter bright, we seize the day!

Half-Bright Heartbeats

Up in the sky, she's peeking through,
Giggling at stars, in shades of blue.
One moment she's shy, the next, she's bold,
A dance of light, like stories told.

She hides behind clouds, just to tease,
Winks at the world with perfect ease.
A playful glimpse, then gone like that,
Our fickle friend, in her silvery hat.

She throws a beam, then pulls it back,
Is she laughing or planning an attack?
Dreaming in shadows, a flicker, a glare,
Sometimes bright, sometimes hardly there.

She'll light up a night with a flash of gold,
Then leave us guessing, her secrets untold.
Yet through her antics, we cherish the light,
Oh, how we love her mischievous flight!

Echoes of Elysium

In the velvet sky, she struts her stuff,
Caught in a mood, is it never enough?
Rolling in laughter, or sulking in blue,
She can't make up her mind, it's so true!

One night a glow, the next a frown,
Swaying through phases, she won't settle down.
A silver diva, in her soft attire,
Mischief and giggles, like sparks from a fire.

She tickles the clouds, gives them a shake,
Her laugh is contagious, make no mistake.
With echoes of joy, she plays hide and seek,
In her moonlit kingdom, she's never weak.

Yet when she's shy, we all feel the dip,
A party with no one, she's missed her trip!
But soon she'll return, in a wild, twinkling spree,
To fill up the night with pure jubilee!

Twilight's Twin Faces

With a wink and a grin, she flashes a smile,
Rocking the twilight, in her own funky style.
One side's a beacon, a guiding bright eye,
The other's a shadow, a whispering sigh.

Bouncing between, a whimsical spree,
Painting the dusk in colors of glee.
A constellation of laughs, a shimmer of tears,
In her twin-faced charm, we let go of fears.

When playful and glowing, she rules the night,
Casting shadows that dance, in pure delight.
But when she's a grump, well, watch your head!
Her playful jeers can fill hearts with dread.

Yet still we love her, in all of her phases,
For every giggle, joy always raises.
A cosmic jester, with tales to share,
In her twilight antics, we find laughter rare!

Phases of the Heartbeat

As she waxes and wanes, she's a sight to behold,
One day she's bold, the next? Shy and cold.
Each twist and each turn, brings laughter and cheer,
A cosmic playmate, so wild and so dear.

It's a comedy show, every night she appears,
With her silver luster and playful jeers.
She rides on the breeze, like a giggling sprite,
Daring us all to join in her flight.

Insolent moods and whimsical pranks,
She'll flood us with light, or leave us in blanks.
Her phases may shift, from calm to a roar,
Like a bouncy ball, she's hard to ignore.

But through every twist, we hold her so tight,
For in her sweet chaos, we find pure delight.
So here's to the lady, who dances above,
In her many moods, we find endless love!

Eclipsed Euphoria

When she hides behind a cloud, oh dear,
A game of peek-a-boo, quite clear.
Giggles echo in the starry night,
While shadows dance, bringing delight.

Now she beams, a silver grin wide,
Winking at lovers, taking them for a ride.
Shooting stars join, in a cosmic jest,
Unruly chaos, a celestial fest.

But wait! A tilt, she spins around,
Her playful antics know no ground.
Chasing rabbits, hopping high,
A luminary of whimsy in the sky.

In slumbers, she dreams of cheese,
Tickling our thoughts, aiming to please.
So here we laugh, under her sway,
As she giggles, night turns to day.

Serenade of Selenites

In the night, they prance and leap,
Underneath the glow, secrets they keep.
With flute-like sounds and tambourines,
Selenites sing of the moon's whimsies, it seems.

They twirl and whirl in silvery light,
Holding hands, they dance in delight.
With starry crowns and laughter so loud,
They whirl up wishes, joyous and proud.

"Look at her shine!" they excitedly cheer,
Yet she flickers, not always sincere.
With a wink and a laugh, she slips from sight,
Leaving behind echoes of night.

Once more, they bounce, climbing the beams,
Their giggles sprinkled within cosmic dreams.
Each lunar mood a reason to sway,
As they celebrate, hip-hip-hooray!

Twilight's Reverie

As twilight grabs her gentle cloak,
She whispers secrets, beneath her folk.
A teasing smile, soft the shades,
Here comes the laughter, in playful glades.

Chasing the sun, she tosses his hat,
Rolling the clouds as if she chats.
Her mood swings, like a game of tag,
One moment bright, the next a brag.

With jittery glows, she lights the way,
While stars snicker in colorful array.
"Is she happy or just in disguise?"
She throws back her head, a laugh that flies.

Leaping through dusk, her charm's unfurled,
Her melodious giggles loop around the world.
Join in the dance, embrace the air,
Twilight's festival, a moment rare.

Craters of Contemplation

In craters deep, where thoughts collide,
She rolls her eyes, full of pride.
"Who needs a mirror?" she lets out a laugh,
Each crater a curve, each bump a gaffe.

With a cosmic sigh, she spins around,
Pondering if jest should wear a crown.
Her whimsies echo the tales of old,
Of farting stars and dreams retold.

"Am I too bright or just a tease?"
She contemplates as night's chill may freeze.
Yet in her heart, a sparkle remains,
A chuckle of joy in those lunar chains.

So let's join in on her hilarious plight,
As she juggles wishes in the moonlight.
Each laughter-filled moment, a wondrous embrace,
In craters of joy, we find our place.

A Radiant Heart in Hiding

When night falls down, she hides with glee,
A cheeky grin only stars can see.
She plays peekaboo behind a cloud,
Whispers secrets to the night so loud.

With every phase, she wears a mask,
Sometimes a smile, at times a task.
Jumping from full to shy retreat,
Her light plays tricks, oh what a feat!

A chuckle bursts as she twirls about,
With playful beams, she shouts out loud.
Leaving shadows dancing on the ground,
In her silver glow, joy can be found.

So when you gaze at her bright face,
Remember, she loves a merry chase.
With each twinkle that lights the night,
She's just a jester, full of delight.

Solitary Glow of the Darkened Night

In solitude, she twirls and spins,
A solo dance, where laughter begins.
To clouds, she winks, a funny little tease,
Her glow brings chuckles, like a gentle breeze.

She dips and dives in a sly ballet,
Chasing birds under the light of rays.
Like a quirky jester in the great expanse,
Her antics make the stars want to dance.

With every flicker, she winks her eye,
Drawing giggles from the night sky.
Each phase she wears, a funny disguise,
A lighthearted jest beneath dark skies.

Oh, how she loves to play her game,
In the theatre of night, she's never the same.
So next time you see her shining bright,
Join in the laughter, it's a curious sight!

Chasing Shadows in Lunar Light

Under silver beams, shadows prance,
A merry chase, a cosmic dance.
With giggles echoing through the trees,
They play tag on the cool night breeze.

A shadow slips, then quickly hides,
In moonlit corners, it slyly slides.
She laughs aloud in radiant mirth,
Celebrating her celestial birth.

As shadows stretch to reach the bright,
A game unfolds in the still of night.
She's the ringmaster, leading the fun,
While shadowy figures whisper and run.

So come and play in her glowing land,
Where shadows tangle like a playful band.
In this lunatic jest of light and dark,
You'll find a joy that leaves its mark!

The Low Tide of Silver Solitude

At low tide, she pulls her fun away,
Gallant reflections start to sway.
With a chuckle, she reveals a shore,
Where secrets hide, and giggles score.

Splashing softly on the sandy scene,
Where dreams and laughter flow unseen.
She tiptoes through the tidal play,
Making shadows giggle all day.

With every rise and gentle fall,
She's cracking jokes; can you hear them all?
A comedic wave that ebbs and flows,
While silver laughter endlessly grows.

So next time you're by the water's edge,
Listen closely, make a pledge.
To join her game, embrace the vibe,
Where solitude and laughter collide!

Starry Soliloquy

In the sky she dons a grin,
With twinkling lights, a routine spin.
One moment shy, the next a tease,
A flicker here, a wink with ease.

Her beams can stretch, then shrink in fright,
Jumping into shadows, avoiding the light.
Chasing clouds like a frisky cat,
"Oh, where's my glow?" she pouts, how's that?

Last night she danced, a full-on show,
Today, she's shy, avoiding the glow.
"Should I shine bright or keep it low?"
She wrestles with her halo's flow.

Like a teen with a crush, oh so bold,
Or a weather talker, timid and cold.
She flips her moods, what's up next?
A sparkle, a giggle, but never vexed.

Flickers of Fantasy

There once was a lady made of light,
Who dressed up in clouds, taking flight.
In one moment, she'd giggle so loud,
The next, she sulked in a silver cloud.

A prankster at heart, she loves a good jest,
"Surprise!" she shouts, "Did I pass your test?"
Hiding behind stars, she plays peek-a-boo,
As night whispers secrets, just me and you.

"Oh look at that!" she cries with glee,
While shooting stars whisper, "Can't you see?"
Her laughter echoes through cosmic trails,
Mixing mischief with her lunar tales.

With a wink and a nod, she pulls her tricks,
Turning the night into playful flicks.
When in doubt, she spins around,
As the sky bursts forth with laughter abound.

Selene's Secrets

In shadows deep, her secrets hide,
With every beam, she takes a ride.
Sometimes bashful, other times bright,
Her moods can change with the fall of night.

"Let's play hide and seek!" she beams so bold,
While starlight giggles, "This never gets old!"
One moment a queen, next moment a sprite,
Spinning her tales in the soft twilight.

"Oh, what a night!" she exclaims with a laugh,
"Do you like my glow? Or should I take a half?"
In shades of silvers and hints of blue,
She jests with the cosmos, a wild crew.

Her luminous spirit can bend to the will,
With every twirl, she gives us a thrill.
A lighthearted muse of laughter they say,
Tickling the dark till the break of day.

Of Night and Nostalgia

With shades of gray and silver bliss,
She swoons and spins in a cosmic kiss.
"Do you remember when we danced last year?"
She giggles softly, "Let's share a cheer!"

Her flashbacks play like old film reels,
With moments of warmth, oh how she feels.
In twilight's glow, she twirls around,
Revisiting laughter, that's where she's found.

A jester of dreams, she winks with flair,
"Was that a tear? Or a spark in the air?"
Then tickles the darkness, a playful jest,
With a glow that reminds us, she's truly blessed.

"Amidst the night, let's dance one more!"
As echoes of laughter, they swirl and soar.
With nostalgia in each flicker and sway,
She shares the joy in her unique way.

Celestial Whispers

In the sky, she grins so wide,
One moment shy, the next, a ride.
Chasing shadows with delight,
Silly games in the deep night.

Her craters giggle, bounce and sway,
Pulling tides, they dance and play.
We laugh at her goofy grace,
As she winks with a shining face.

Round and round, she spins her tale,
Feeling joy, then feeling pale.
Jumping from bright to barely there,
In her light, we shed our care.

She peeks shyly behind a cloud,
Then shines, yelling, "Look at me, crowd!"
A lunar tease, a playful jest,
In her glow, we feel so blessed.

Night's Changing Face

Up high, she wears a silly grin,
Then pouts, saying, "Let the games begin!"
With phases shifting, feeling spry,
One minute bright, the next, awry.

Her laughter echoes in the night,
Turning shadows into fright.
"Oh dear," she sighs, "what should I do?"
"Maybe a jig under stars so blue?"

Just when we think she's had her fun,
She hides away, plays on the run.
Her face changes with a wink,
In daylight, she's gone – so quick, you blink!

How she pulls us in her charm,
With every giggle, there's no harm.
From curvy crescent to full-on glee,
With each bright laugh, she's wild and free.

Reflections in Silver

Glistening down like a playful tease,
  She throws a party on the breeze.
Splashes of silver, twinkling bright,
  Casting shadows, a funny sight.

"Oh dear," she says, "where's my dress?"
"Oops, I'm bare, but I must confess!"
  With a chuckle, she spins around,
  In her glow, joy can be found.

Each trickster beam holds a chat,
"What's this, a mouse? No, just a cat!"
  Telling secrets to the stars,
  Blowing wishes to the Mars.

A silver laugh, a glowing grin,
Where does her playfulness begin?
In every twinkling light she shares,
  Her silly spirit dances, flares.

Phases of the Heart

She wears her moods, a fickle heart,
One moment bold, then plays it smart.
A shining arc, a dip, a dive,
"Can't catch me," she sings alive!

When she's full, all seem so bright,
Then shrinks a bit, hides from the light.
"Oh, come on!" we groan in cheer,
"Stay awhile, don't disappear!"

With each new phase, a different song,
A giggle here, a laugh so strong.
A sky-bound diva in her way,
Leading our dreams where we can play.

So here's to her, our silver muse,
In every phase, we can't refuse.
A playful soul with many parts,
She spins and twirls, our joyful hearts.

Whirling Galaxies of Experience

Up in the sky, round and bright,
She dances with stars, a comical sight.
One minute she's shy, the next she's a tease,
Her laughter spreads joy, like a warm summer breeze.

With a wink to the sun, she'd spin and twirl,
In a cosmic playground, giving dreams a whirl.
Tickling the planets, making them chuckle,
Turning dull nights into a stellar huddle.

Her glow shifts in hues, a playful delight,
Sometimes she's full, sometimes just a bite.
Swapping her costumes from silver to gray,
She keeps the universe guessing all day.

Oh, how she jests with her light and shade,
Creating a spectacle that never will fade.
A cosmic comedian, bringing smiles evermore,
With whirls of experience, she's never a bore.

Evocative Echoes in the Night Air

Listen, the night brings whispers of cheer,
Bouncing off craters, drifting so near.
She chuckles and giggles, a bright silver chime,
Filling the darkness with humor and rhyme.

When shadows play tricks, she beams with glee,
Lighting up moments, wild and free.
Joking with comets, flirting with light,
Her laughter outshines the philosophical night.

A prankster at heart, she'll make shadows dance,
Inviting starlight to join in her prance.
With every glimmer, she mutters and teases,
Crafting each moment into shimmering breezes.

From dusk until dawn, her giggles resonate,
Echoing softly, they frolic and prate.
Turning the night into a carnival spree,
With evocative echoes, she's jolly and free.

Visions of Night and Day

In twilight's embrace, she paints quite the scene,
With brushstrokes of laughter, lovely and keen.
Shimmering doubts are swept far away,
In her whimsical world, it's always a play.

From dusk 'til dawn, she flirts with the skies,
In a game of hide-and-seek, where laughter flies.
The stars join her antics, each prancer and twirler,
While shooting stars dress up as a funny whirler.

What a sight to behold, those visions at night,
When dreams mix with giggles, igniting delight.
Oh, morning may come with gentle surprises,
But she leaves us with joy, in delightful disguises.

As day breaks anew, her chuckles remain,
In memories spun with the laughter and change.
With each turning phase, a story to say,
In visions of wonder, she brightens the gray.

Craters of Yearning and Echoes

In craters of longing, she stirs up the fun,
Amusing her audience, each and every one.
With shadows that dance and twinkle with glee,
She turns our heart aches to a whimsical spree.

"Oh dear, where's my glow?" she giggles and sighs,
As shadows play hide-and-seek in the skies.
Poking at dreams, she crafts silly schemes,
Making wishes spin like confetti in beams.

With echoes resounding, she throws back her head,
In laughter that tumbles, nothing feels dread.
Lighting her playhouse with cosmic delight,
She banters with stardust throughout the night.

Each crater holds tales of longing and joy,
Her playful demeanor, a sweet, shining ploy.
In playful mosaics, she teaches us how,
With echoes of laughter, we dance in the now.

Gleaming Whimsy in Midnight's Grip

In the quiet night, she grins wide,
Dancing with shadows she won't hide.
Playing peek-a-boo with the stars,
Making wishes on swirling jars.

Her face a canvas, painted bright,
Spinning giggles through silver light.
One moment coy, the next a tease,
A mischievous sprite, with laughter keys.

She winks at the owls, they hoot in glee,
A jester of night, so wild and free.
Her beams twinkle like a child's eyes,
In the haven where bright joy lies.

Mirth swirls around her, a shining orb,
Crafting a jest that the night can absorb.
With every phase, a comic play,
In her glowing presence, the shadows sway.

The Paradox of Celestial Stillness.

Floating in silence, she's sly as a fox,
Nibbling on starlight, it's all in the box.
One moment she's calm, the next she'll dive,
A giggly enigma, she's very alive.

Her beams drape low, then soar up high,
Like a balloon that can't decide how to fly.
She flickers and flirts, a tease in the night,
With a wink and a smirk, she's a marvelous sight.

Her pull's like a prank, with tides to unfold,
Whispering secrets in silver and gold.
A push and a pull, she giggles atop,
In the dance of the universe, she won't stop.

Amusing the waves, creating a show,
Rolling on laughter, with each ebb and flow.
A playful reminder, no way to resist,
When she's out and about, there's joy to persist.

Lunar Laughter

Chasing the shadows, she giggles and beams,
A motley of moods in the night's silly dreams.
With a grin that can light a thousand glades,
Her laughter echoes, through moonbeam cascades.

She frolics with clouds, plays hide and seek,
Tickling the night like a cosmic freak.
Each twinkle a grin, each shimmer a jest,
In the comedy of night, she is the best.

Her whims whisk the tides, a playful decree,
Making waves dance like they're laughing with glee.
She rolls with the tides, a celestial jest,
And spreads her cheer, inviting the rest.

In this jovial sky, her humor unfolds,
With each rising phase, a story retold.
To the world down below, she sends her delight,
In lunar laughter, oh what a sight!

Tides of Emotion

A capricious queen in a sky full of jest,
Her beams brush the waves, never letting them rest.
One moment serene, the next in a whirl,
Her mood swings like tides, an enchanting twirl.

She giggles with fishermen, glows in their nets,
Crafting jokes with the breezes, no regrets.
With ebbing and flowing, her laughter's the key,
Unlocking the night with whimsical glee.

Frogs sing her praises in croaks loud and clear,
Winking at crickets, she draws them near.
Her joy is contagious, spinning around,
In the tide of emotions, hilarity's found.

Bobbing like boats on her shimmering skin,
Whispers of laughter where night may begin.
Each phase tells a tale, each ray has a twist,
In the vast ocean of night, she reigns with a tryst.

Craters of Joy and Sorrow

In the night sky she giggles, a silly old friend,
Her craters, like laughter, that twist and bend.
Sometimes she winks, with a mischievous glee,
Other times she sulks, quite dramatically.

Twirling in shadows, a dance gone awry,
One moment she sparkles, the next she could cry.
A halo of joy, then a frown comes to play,
Each peek-a-boo phase keeps the stargazers gray.

In daylight she hides, peeking just a bit,
With giggles of silver, she doesn't quite quit.
A tease for the suns that claim all the light,
She throws them a wink, then hides out of sight.

Oh, what a whirl, in her cratered delight,
From giggles to grumbles, she sparkles so bright.
With phases that change like a comedy scene,
Our nighttime comedian, the celestial queen.

Shaded Radiance

In the glow of the night, she plays hide and seek,
With shadows and laughter, her tactics are sleek.
One moment a beacon, all bubbly and spry,
Then somberly sighing, a tear in her eye.

The stars roll their eyes at her whimsical tricks,
As she casts her bright spells, then pulls out her kicks.
When giggles get caught in her wax and wane,
It's a cosmic ballet—what a humorous strain!

Through beams of delight, she folds into gloom,
A drama unfolds in the darkened room.
With phases that flirt and then suddenly freeze,
She lightens the heaviness just with a tease.

Oh, shaded radiance, madcap and bright,
You've got all the skies laughing deep into night.
With your lovable antics that nobody shuns,
You're the jesting celestial, outshining the suns!

Flickering Phases

Oh flickering friend, are you laughing or sad?
In one little glance, you're a little bit mad!
With a chuckle of light, you play tricks from above,
Then sulking in shadows, you flee from our love.

A twinkling trickster, with moods that can flip,
One moment you're graceful, next, a clown's grip.
Your phases parade in a daring ballet,
A comedy show that leaves us in dismay!

Sometimes you're cheeky, a playful delight,
Other times you vanish, a true ghost of night.
With beams you are radiant, in darkness you tease,
Hiding your joy with the greatest of ease.

So here's to your flickers, imperfect and bright,
You turn our cosmos into laughter and light.
A starry affair with the quirkiest frown,
Our joyous companion, with silver polka-dots crown!

Dreamlike Drift

In the velvet expanse, dreams drift and play,
With whims of delight that sway night into day.
One minute she shimmers, a pearl on the sea,
Next, hiding her laughter, as coy as can be.

Drifting like whispers, in and out of our sight,
A jester at heart, she juggles the night.
Sometimes she's frolicking, all sparkles and cheer,
Then tucking away, as if hiding in fear.

Oh, to catch her grinning, that canvas so wide,
With phases all pirouetting, where do we confide?
From joyful jubilation to shadowy gloom,
A dreamlike drift dances, a playful costume.

So here's to the night, your antics, we'll cheer,
With beams that are giggles, we hold you so dear.
You twirl in the sky, a delightful charade,
Our wondrous companion, in moonlight parade.

Luna's Kaleidoscope of Feelings

Up high she beams with pride,
While hiding behind clouds she'll hide.
In a wink, she's coy and shy,
Then suddenly, she starts to fly.

She giggles with a twinkle bright,
And sulks when clouds dim her light.
A whimsical dance, a playful tease,
Her laughter echoes through the trees.

With each phase, she takes a spin,
A cheeky grin beneath her skin.
Her whims like ribbons in the air,
A lively show, beyond compare.

When grumpy, she'll just frown and pout,
And cast a shadow, roundabout.
But soon enough, she'll prance and play,
Changing shapes throughout the day.

A Silver Lining of Secrets

She peeks from shadows, sly and clear,
In a wink, she draws you near.
A silver lining to reveal,
With giggles wrapped in starlit steel.

Sometimes she twirls, a dazzling sight,
Other times scowls, and dims the night.
Whispers secrets in a beam,
As if playing with a moonlit dream.

Her laughter ripples through the night,
Casting spells with pure delight.
A capricious sprite, she'll glide and slide,
With a cosmic smile that can't abide.

Each glowing phase, a chuckle shared,
Her antics leave the heavens bared.
A playful tease, a mischievous shout,
In her silver light, there's never doubt.

Symphony of Stars and Solitude

Amidst the stars, a song she sings,
With twinkling notes that joyfully bring.
She waltzes with the shadows near,
While sharing secrets, soft and clear.

A solemn face, she wears at times,
Yet bursts with laughter, jester of climes.
Her mood swings like the tides at play,
In the symphony of night's ballet.

When grumpy clouds dare block her face,
She throws a dance, a wild embrace.
Then prancing back, she takes the stage,
With cheeky jests for every age.

In radiant glow, she casts her spell,
A serenade the stars know well.
A sly wink to the lonely night,
In her merry tales, we find delight.

The Duality of Night's Embrace

One moment bright, the next demure,
Her mood swings, a playful lure.
With every glance, her face will change,
A cosmic dance, so wild and strange.

She might be coy, a ghostly smile,
Then burst with joy and waltz a mile.
In giggles and sighs, she spins around,
With stardust laughter in leaps unbound.

On somber nights, she might just pout,
And throw her beams, a playful clout.
But lighter hearts, she loves to tease,
With glimmers that flutter on the breeze.

A silent jester in skies of blue,
Her duality, a riddle few knew.
With every phase, she takes her flight,
Bringing joy and wonder to the night.

www.ingramcontent.com/pod-product-compliance
Lightning Source LLC
Chambersburg PA
CBHW051646160426
43209CB00004B/811